*Nigel C*

# Homelessness and Evangelism

### Ralph Upton CA

Housing and Homelessness Officer,
Liverpool Diocesan Board for Social Responsibility

## GROVE BOOKS LIMITED
RIDLEY HALL RD  CAMBRIDGE  CB3 9HU

# Contents

**Acknowledgements**
I would like to thank Ultan Russell for his help and encouragement
while writing this booklet and Irene Summers for her work on the text.

**The Cover Illustration** is by Peter Ashton

---

# Church Army and the Grove Evangelism Series

Church Army has over 350 evangelists working in five areas of focus, at the cutting edge of evangelism in the UK. It co-sponsors the publication of the Grove Evangelism Series as part of its aim of stimulating discussion about evangelism strategies, and sharing its experience of front-line evangelism.

Further details about Church Army are available from:
Church Army, Independents Road, Blackheath, London SE3 9LG.
Telephone: 020 8 318 1226. Fax: 020 8 318 5258.
Registered charity number: 226226

---

**First Impression** November 2000
**ISSN** 1367-0840
**ISBN** 1 85174 449 5

# 1
# Introduction

*Definitions and Statistics*

Homelessness is a far wider problem than just not 'having a roof over your head.' We all need a place where we feel safe and able to relax. It is difficult to estimate the number of homeless people in Britain, but around 55,000 households were accepted as homeless at the end of 1999.

Defining homelessness is far from easy. I adopt the definition that homeless people are individuals or families socially excluded from lasting occupancy of a suitable dwelling and who:
- are without shelter,
- find shelter through temporary accommodation, in an institution, or with relatives or friends,
- are subject to unacceptable housing conditions.

Families become homeless for a variety of reasons, such as redundancy, marriage breakdown, illness or the termination of a tenancy, and should be dealt with as a family group.

Local authorities have to make an assessment of whether a household is homeless. To meet the criteria you must prove that you have not made yourself 'intentionally homeless' and you must be in priority need, which means you are vulnerable, due perhaps to age, disability or having dependent children.

The hidden problem is enormous; some people stay with relatives in overcrowded accommodation or sleep on a friend's floor or settee. Some, who have had either a bad experience of the system or know the system well enough to know they do not qualify, do not bother to present themselves; thus they are not included in any figures.

*Reasons for Homelessness*

It is hard to identify the main reasons for homelessness. Until relationships have been formed people will not open up and tell you their real problems. So often what is presented as the reason for a person being homeless is not the reason at all, but rather one of convenience.

The following figures, taken from the Government's Housing Green Paper (2000), illustrate some of the reasons for people becoming homeless:
- 20% of people leaving care are likely to become homeless in the next two years;
- a quarter to a third of rough sleepers have been 'in care' as children;
- Shelter had more than 1,000 calls last year from women fleeing violence;
- Shelterline took 3,655 calls from 16- and 17-year-olds in its first year. Of these, 80% were homeless, and over half were street homeless;
- a study of young homeless people showed that 86% had been forced to leave home and had not chosen to do so;

- half of those who were sleeping rough had been in a prison or remand centre at some time;
- a quarter of those sleeping rough had been in the armed forces at some time.

Sir David Ramsbotham, Her Majesty's Chief Inspector of Prisons, stated in an article for the Spring 2000 *Home and Family* magazine, that 34% of young offenders had been through the care system and that 11% of offenders were evicted from home before the age of fifteen. This supports the argument that there is a major link between homelessness and crime. Sir David goes on to state that released prisoners have three needs: a home, a job and a stable environment. This surely applies equally to a homeless person.

### Government Response

The Government has appointed a 'homelessness czar' to head up its strategy, and has made minor changes to legislation.

The Government published its strategy *Coming in from the Cold* in December 1999, followed in January 2000 by a companion document, *Coming in from the Cold: Delivering the Strategy*. To back this up it announced a Special Innovation Fund to support innovative work in the field of practical work to help prevent rough sleeping.

In April 2000 the Government published its Green Paper on Housing called *Quality and Choice*[1] which, according to Shelter, was the most significant opportunity there has been for a generation to tackle homelessness. Among the proposals is a duty on local authorities to provide long-term accommodation for homeless families, and a licensing scheme for local landlords who let out shared properties, in order to improve safety and quality.

The Government also proposes to give more priority to those who are most at risk of becoming homeless, including those leaving care, those being released from prison, women fleeing domestic violence and 16- and 17-year-olds. If these proposals are put in place then they will prevent a lot of people from ending up homeless.

### Social Housing

In the Green Paper, the Government states that there is now significantly less social housing available. There are now one million fewer dwellings owned by local authorities and social landlords than there were in 1977. This is partly due to the 'right to buy' schemes in which 1.6 million local authority homes were sold off between 1979 and 1999. The effect is less housing available for the poorest and most vulnerable group of people in our society.

Some local councils do claim to have plenty of housing available, but it tends to be in hard to let areas with a number of social problems such as drug dealing, vandalism and other crime. The Government states that it wants to address these

---

1  *The Housing Green Paper: Quality and Choice* (Dept of the Environment, Transport and the Regions, 2000).

problems, and sets out the following questions as a basis for action:
- Who should social housing be for and on what terms?
- How should it be provided and funded?
- What should be the scale and location of future social housing developments?
- How should it relate to other forms of housing?
- How can we avoid the stigmatization and ghettoization of social housing?
- How can we turn it into a housing solution instead of a housing problem?

This is obviously looking at long-term solutions rather than the short term, and the church has a role to play. This booklet looks at a Christian response to homelessness, with some practical examples of how local churches have responded.

## Young People

Many young people do not fit into the usual definitions of homelessness. Benefits for young people do little to help the situation, as those under the age of 25 only receive what is known as 'single room rent.' They receive only the average cost of a shared house rather than self-contained accommodation. This means they are financially disadvantaged, coupled with which they can end up sharing with people with drug or alcohol problems or who have a tendency to be violent, putting a very vulnerable group in danger.

Shelter have published a booklet entitled *Young People and Homelessness*, and they quote from a report by the National Inquiry into Preventing Youth Homelessness stating that at least 246,000 young people became homeless in 1995. They continue by stating that a quarter of single homeless people are sleeping rough, living in hostels or in bed-and-breakfast accommodation.

## Asylum Seekers

When looking at homelessness, we cannot ignore the plight of asylum seekers, many of whom are living in sub-standard accommodation and with cultural and language problems.

On behalf of the Bishop and the Board for Social Responsibility in Liverpool I have worked closely with key agencies on pastoral care of asylum seekers and refugees. This is a specialist problem, needing a specific approach, which is beyond the scope of this booklet. However, the church's contribution to this area at national and regional level is significant.

# 2
# A Christian Response

## Theology of Homelessness

Jesus very much identified with the poor and those on the edge of society. Mary and Joseph arrived in Bethlehem, and could find nowhere to stay, so Jesus was born in a dirty smelly stable. The modern equivalent could easily be a derelict building or a squat in one of our cities.

Isaiah 52 and 53 are widely accepted as referring to Jesus. He was despised and rejected, a man of sorrows, anguish and tears and he became the crucified one. In Matthew 25 Jesus identifies with those on the very edge of society. We are told that whenever we carry out an act of kindness for the least of these we are doing it for him, and judgment will fall on those who do not care for this group of people. Even though he was the Son of God, Jesus was prepared to make himself nothing and to take on the very nature of a servant (Philippians 2).

Throughout the ministry of Jesus we see how he lived among the poor and spoke out against injustice. Jesus lived among the poor for a long time before his ministry here began. If we are to follow this example it is very challenging. Relatively speaking, the church is not poor, and Christians are reasonably well-off. This is an incarnational theology that would cause the church to make a huge shift from a gathered community to one that is more of a missionary model of being church.

Sadly, the reaction to a homeless person on our streets or at the back of church is often to ignore them, yet Jesus was very critical of those who did not show love and concern for those in need (Luke 11.46). He is very critical of those who pay more attention to the law than to caring for people.

Jesus himself chose an itinerant ministry and relied on people to provide him with shelter, and when he sent out the disciples he told them to travel light, taking no purse. In all of this Jesus identified with the homeless.

There is nothing explicit in the Bible about the right of a person to a home, but there is much about justice and caring for those in need.

## The Church as a Prophetic Voice

When I took up my new role as Housing and Homelessness Officer, I asked Christian and secular organizations what they thought I could bring to the work that was going on amongst homeless people. Generally the Christian organizations mentioned funding, volunteers and education, while a number of the secular organizations wanted me to get the church to use its voice to speak out against the injustice of homelessness and poverty. They recognized that the church still had a voice that was listened to wherever power might rest. It seems to me that Christians greatly underestimate what effect the voice of the church can have.

It must not, though, be overused, or I fear it could just become yet another voice trying to make itself heard amongst many other voices.

There are, I believe, several ways we can do this. The buzz-word of the moment is 'partnership,' so the church should not be afraid to get involved in the various groups that are being set up, and to work together with those who share our agenda.

The church needs to acknowledge the importance of networking effectively and efficiently, both with other Christian groups that are working in the area of homelessness and also with secular organizations. In this way the prophetic voice of the church can be the salt in a number of different areas.

Often Christian professionals are already working in voluntary and statutory agencies for the homeless. More could be done by the church community to support them and give them the confidence to speak out.

More use could be made of the media. Christians working in the field of homelessness could write to newspapers on areas of concern. Homelessness Sunday, promoted through many Christian organizations like Church Action on Poverty and the Churches National Housing Coalition, is a valuable tool for raising awareness. The Bishop of Guildford, The Rt Revd John Gladwin, made a statement in January 2000 just prior to Homelessness Sunday, and he used quite strong words, stating the following:

> The church has a fundamental responsibility towards those who are excluded from the mainstream of society. You cannot get much more excluded than being without a home and forced to live on the streets, particularly in the depth of winter. There is no romance in being poor, cold, in need and without a home. Whether you are young, middle-aged or elderly, living on the streets is degrading, dehumanizing and a frighteningly vulnerable place to be. We are all called to respond.

These words are a strong reminder to all of us that these problems must be taken seriously. Not only can Homelessness Sunday be the theme of worship but it could also be used as an educational tool in relation to schools and the media. I was asked to plan a series of 'Thoughts for the day' on Radio Merseyside during the week following on from Homelessness Sunday.

Senior clergy often have access to council and government officials, and perhaps more use could be made of this to promote Christian values without fear and to enable decision-makers to be challenged. In April 2000 the Bishop of Croydon, the Rt Revd Wilfred Wood, spoke out on the hysteria surrounding the asylum seekers. He said that there had been 'a stirring up of racism and bigotry, and that black people's peace of mind does not figure very high in our politicians' list of priorities.' Speaking out in this way for the weak is what we are called to do as Christians, yet so often we have remained silent.

The Church of England is most fortunate to have bishops sitting in the House of Lords. They are able to speak out on a variety of issues and make the Christian voice heard at the centre of decision-making. Probably the best example of this was the *Faith in the City* report, in which the church took a stand against the policies of the government at that time. It is imperative that those of us who are involved in homelessness work continue to keep the bishops well briefed on the current issues so they can make the most of this opportunity.

Those ministering and working with the homeless suffer high stress levels and often witness quite distressing scenes. The church needs to offer support to these people.

## Evangelizing Homeless People

I recently put on an evangelistic event in a Christian drop-in centre. It was on a night when the centre would not normally be open and it was made clear what was going on. There was a buffet, so it could be argued that there was 'bait.'

A clergyman was most indignant with me over this, saying that I had no right to evangelize homeless people. I suspect that the church would divide on this, but we do need to consider this issue in an objective manner.

If we look at the ministry of Jesus, it is true to say that with the exception of the twelve, there is little evidence of Jesus telling anyone to follow him, but he did challenge all people, both rich and poor, with kingdom values. He also spent a lot of his time with the people on the edge of society, healing the blind, the lepers, beggars and setting people free of evil spirits.

The Great Commission makes it clear that Jesus does not differentiate between one group of people and another: 'Therefore go and make disciples of all nations, baptizing them in the name of the Father and of the Son and of the Holy Spirit' (Matthew 28.19). However you read this, it is inclusive. All people have the right to hear the gospel, but the task of making disciples must always be done with sensitivity.

The question that we ask ourselves is, 'why do we engage in work with homeless people?'

I find John Stott very helpful on this subject. In his book *Christian Mission in the Modern World* he identifies three ways of looking at the link between evangelism and social action:

1. Social action is a means to evangelism and nothing more; the winning of converts is the aim;
2. Social action is a manifestation of evangelism or of the gospel which is being proclaimed—in this model social action creates the opportunity to preach the gospel;
3. Social action is a partner of evangelism—they belong to each other but are independent.[2]

The first model is very hard to defend and I would suggest this is a cynical view of Christian social action. Gandhi quite rightly asked, 'Why should I become a

2   John Stott, *Christian Mission in the Modern World* (Kingsway Publications, 1986).

Christian simply because the doctor who treats me happens to be one?'

The second model has more to commend it as long as the action is borne out of a genuine love for the person who is in need. The third model is the one that I support. If someone is hungry and sleeping rough, food and shelter are his or her main needs at that time. When we see a fellow human being in that sort of situation then the love for our neighbour should move us to action. We should not forget that Jesus reminds us that what we do for the least of these brothers and sisters we are doing for him (Matthew 25.31ff).

But if a homeless person shares a spiritual problem with us or asks us about why we are helping them, then do we not have a duty to share with them the good news of the gospel?

Therefore I believe that it is right in certain circumstances to share the gospel with a homeless person, with the aim of challenging them to accept Jesus as Lord and Saviour.

## 3
# Practical Responses

If as Christians we want the right to speak out on these issues then first we must demonstrate that we care enough to get our hands dirty. In society today many people have become resistant to words, and all too often the commitment of the word has not been carried out. Prayer should be central to all that we as Christians do, but it is not enough or acceptable to tell someone in need that we will pray for them. John Stott, in his book *New Issues Facing Christians Today*,[3] speaks about a woman who went to a local vicar for help. When she was told he was busy and would pray for her, she wrote a poem, which she passed to Shelter:

> *I was hungry, and you formed a humanities group to discuss my hunger.*
> *I was imprisoned, and you crept off quietly to your chapel to pray for my release.*
> *I was naked, and in your mind you debated the morality of my appearance.*
> *I was sick, and you knelt and thanked God for your health.*
> *I was homeless, and you preached to me of the spiritual shelter of the love of God.*
> *I was lonely, and you left me alone to pray for me.*
> *You seem so holy, so close to God but I am still very hungry—and lonely—and cold.*

I suspect that as some of us read this poem it makes us feel uncomfortable as we recognize ourselves in it. Often we can be the answer to our own prayer by responding in a practical way, and we will be looking at some examples of this in later chapters.

### Callers at the Door/People on the Street

Often our first contact with homeless people will be with callers at the door, either at the church or the minister's home, and as highlighted in this poem some practical action is needed. This does not mean, though, that in our urgency to help all else goes out of the window, because our own safety must also be considered. Often the request will be for money or somewhere to sleep. It is useful to have a checklist to hand:

- Do not give cash.
- Have food and drink available.
- Have a list of local direct access hostels and other service providers to hand
- Shelter often have a Local Accommodation Directory, available for a small fee.
- Have a notice on an outside wall saying that money is not given. An example of this can be found at the vicarage at St Helens, Sandal Magna in the Diocese of Wakefield:

3   John Stott, *New Issues Facing Christians Today* (Marshall Pickering, 1999) pp 23–24.

> Welcome to the Vicarage
>
> Visitors are more than welcome to talk through a
> problem or ask for prayer, but it is not our policy to
> give money to anyone.
>
> Thank you for calling.

For further reading on this subject there is a Grove Booklet *Responding to Callers* by John Hall.[4]

*Do Your Research*

When people call at the door, what we are doing is reacting to the need presented to us, but we may feel that we want to be more pro-active in responding to the needs of the homeless. If so, it is most important to do effective research before embarking upon any course of action.

Speak to the local authority and the various homeless agencies in the area to ensure that what you propose is needed, and find out if there are any plans by anyone else to set up a similar project. If there are, perhaps you could work with them on this.

Some Christians may feel uncomfortable with the idea of working with non-Christians on a project because their motivation may be different. Raymond Fung, in his book *The Isaiah Vision*, sets out a shared agenda in which those of a Christian faith and other people of different faiths or no faith, can work together:[5]

* Children do not die
* Old people live in dignity
* Those who plant vineyards eat the fruit of their labour

This is based on Isaiah's vision (Isaiah 65.20–23) of a restored community in which all people find fulfilment and people do not labour in vain but enjoy the results of their labour. It is with this in mind that a strategy can be set up in partnership with other people pursuing this shared agenda. The intention is to get involved with other groups of people, and whilst working with them, to share by word and deed the message of the gospel.

In the process of working towards the Isaiah vision the people should grow to know and understand one another and to break down barriers. This gives another dimension to our evangelism, because not only are we reaching out to homeless

4    John Hall, *Responding to Callers* (Grove Pastoral booklet P 79).
5    Raymond Fung, *The Isaiah Vision* (WCC Publications, 1991).

people but it is also a means of challenging our partners with the Christian faith, encouraging them to follow Christ and to become members of the Christian community.

## Be Equipped

As well as doing our research outside, we need to be honest as we look at our church, asking the question: 'Have we got the expertise to get involved in this work?' Often individuals and churches get into trouble by moving into an area of work without fully weighing up what may be involved. It would be wise to do a lot of research about what you are becoming involved in.

Also it must be remembered that whatever work we engage in will cost money, and it may be that we cannot afford to finance such a project. Funding may need to be sought for this piece of work. If we do not have the expertise to seek funding ourselves, the church headquarters or the local Council for Voluntary Service (CVS) could be contacted for help. Rural Community Councils may be able to help in some areas.

# 4
# Soup Run and Outreach

Louise Casey, the Government's 'homelessness czar,' stated that this country's culture of kindness was simply keeping people on the streets, and was very critical of soup runs for this reason. Paul Bracchi, a *Daily Mail* reporter, went underground in London to see if this was true. In an article of the 27 November 1999 he suggested that there were probably too many soup runs, and people chose which one to feed from, but he also noted that some people slip through the net due to bad co-ordination.

In his article Bracchi described how he tried to get a bed in a hostel but all were full, and how at one stage he felt he was in danger of attack. In the back of his mind was the statistic that homeless people are fifty times more likely than anyone else to die of a violent assault. He describes how difficult it was to keep warm in the biting cold and the dejection felt by those around him. This led Paul Bracchi to conclude his article by stating that rather than keeping people on the streets, soup runs were simply keeping them alive.

This confirms the need for good research before we embark on a new project. It is obvious there is a need, but how we respond is open to negotiation.

Once the need for a soup run has been established there is no doubt that it is a good way of reaching out and meeting with people where they are and to offer basic needs.

## The Excluded

There has been a lot of debate about people begging on the streets. It has to be recognized that some are in genuine need but a substantial number are not homeless or are sleeping in hostels. Street begging gives them the means to support a drug habit, and with other means begging can bring in a substantial figure—one local authority has suggested a figure between £500 and £800 a week.

*Big Issue* sellers are the other visible face of homelessness. Some of the vendors use the money they make for drugs or alcohol, but others do use the money to get themselves in to accommodation.

I cannot tell people whether they should purchase the *Big Issue* or not, but people do have to prove they are homeless before they can become *Big Issue* sellers. Standing on a cold street corner selling the magazine is not an easy option, and it at least gives a little order to a chaotic lifestyle. People should also be aware that the Big Issue Trust has initiated programmes and projects to work with the vendors, helping them to gain access to medical services, to take the step from selling the *Big Issue* to doing other work, and to find accommodation and resettlement support. This is not available if a person is not badged up and selling the *Big Issue*.

Some people live on the streets by choice. They do not want to be tied down by rules and regulations or they may feel vulnerable to attack, and, in their opinion, to live on the streets and sleep rough is preferable and safer than sleeping in a hostel.

Others may not choose to live on the streets, but suffer from drug and alcohol addiction and mental health problems. Some can be violent and may have been banned from hostels because their lifestyle poses a risk to staff and other residents. To this group of people, outreach workers and soup runs are a lifeline and perhaps the only real contact they have with the rest of society.

### The Small Church

Even a small church with limited resources of money and personnel can respond to the problem of homelessness. A good example of this is St Bride's Church in Liverpool. This church has a very small congregation but a large, centrally positioned and well-equipped church building ideal for hosting both a soup run and a drop-in.

Students from Liverpool John Moores University's Student Community Action had done a soup run for a number of years. In autumn 1999 they lost their accommodation, so an approach was made to St Bride's, which now acts as a host for the project. This would have been impossible to resource from the church congregation. On one night the students go out onto the street to serve soup, but later in the week food is served in the church building, bringing over thirty people through the doors of the church and thus offering the opportunity for Christians to build relationships with the homeless community.

This has had the effect of bringing not only the homeless community into contact with the church but also the students and other volunteers. It provides an opportunity for sharing the Christian faith in word and deed with all those who are involved with the project. It would also appear to be quite a radical shift from a church struggling to keep its head above water to one that is following the example of Jesus and becoming incarnational among the people and relevant to the society around it. One of the service users recently said to the vicar that it was so good for him to allow his church to be used. And it has allowed people to remember their own involvement with the church in the past and may be a start to bringing the flickering flame of faith back to life.

The church members were quite apprehensive at first, but since the project has been running there has been a change of attitude in the church as homeless people have now got a name and an identity.

### The Large Church

Frontline Church in Liverpool is a large independent evangelical church with good resources of people and finance. They operate a soup run with no need to enter into a partnership. Chris Rice has been involved in this work since 1988, first at another church in Anfield and then at Frontline since 1990. Chris remembers walking into a burnt-out club and finding at least fifteen people sleeping there. At that time God told him he would always have a heart for these people.

14

There are a total of sixty volunteers, who operate on a rota basis, with a minimum of six people at a time for security reasons. They go out three nights a week. A lot of human resources are needed to operate in this way. New volunteers are always needed; those who apply have an informal interview at which they are told what they are getting into, as well as the sorts of things to do and not do. The training itself, though, takes place on the job, learning from those who are experienced in the work.

The people they come into contact with have many different needs, including a variety of medical problems such as HIV/Aids, hepatitis, lacerations, mental health problems and drug and alcohol problems, so the team needs to be equipped to handle these either directly or by referral. This highlights the need to be linked to other agencies. For people on drugs there can be long waiting lists for detoxification, but a Christian organization may be able to respond sooner and so provide more effective help.

## Starting Up

I asked Chris what advice he could give to anyone thinking of starting up a soup run. He said the following points should be considered:

- There should be vision and conviction, not a response out of condemnation. If God is telling you to do it you will know.
- Teams should be a minimum of five for safety reasons.
- Prayer support is paramount.
- Be regular, on the same night each week. If you are inconsistent your motives will be questioned.
- Volunteers need to be carefully selected.
- Do not proclaim the gospel unless asked.
- Be prepared to touch the untouchable.

## The 'Soup Kitchen Church'

When the service users ask the providers why they are running the soup kitchen it is then that they share their faith. Chris was known as part of the drug scene and so his story of how he came to faith is very powerful. It is obviously an advantage if you have someone like this, but I would say if you have reached this stage, you already have credibility with your listeners.

Chris told me that he saw the soup kitchen as his church. He saw it as a form of cell church actually on the streets with himself as the Pastor. They break bread together, which I thought was a powerful picture of believers being a body without a church building. This raised questions in my mind about discipling and pastoral care, which ultimately is overcome by meeting in cafés. Frontline has a café of its own, so some go there. However, at some stage something a little more structured is needed, but it would appear that attending the main church is not a major barrier.

I suspect that a lot of the barriers have already been overcome by the fact that the service users know a number of the church members. Thus the transition from cell group to mother church should be a lot easier. Another relevant point which Chris made, is that those who come from prison often know a lot about Jesus even if they do not know him personally, and they may have attended prison chapel so church services are not totally alien to them.

## Work Experience

As part of the rehabilitation process, Frontline give people work to do at the church. This would seem to fulfil a number of needs:

- it helps them to feel a part of the church, loved and accepted and gives them worth;
- it gets them away from former peers and peer pressure and surrounds them with support;
- it gets them into the habit of working, as an interim stage to New Deal.

## Overview

To feed someone would appear to be meeting a very basic need, and Jesus aligns himself with people in this situation. Matthew 25 tells us it is he who is the thirsty, the prisoner, the stranger, the naked, the homeless, the sick, the dying, the oppressed and the humiliated. To go out onto the street in this way is to respond as Jesus tells us we should. At the same time, Jesus warns us that if we do not do these things it is him that we are turning our back on.

# 5
# Drop-in Centres

'The ROC' in St Helens started about nine years ago, when a group of people from the churches in St Helens decided they wished to respond to the plight of the homeless community by serving soup and sandwiches on a council car park in the town centre.

This progressed, and they started to do an 'Open Christmas,' funded by Crisis and other charities until about four years ago. The Council then allowed them to take over a Council-owned property on a peppercorn rent, and at present they open three nights a week plus an 'open Christmas.' Hence the name ROC—'Relief over Christmas.' The exciting thing about this project is that it is truly ecumenical and is managed and resourced by lay people. In April 2000 a full-time worker was appointed and other professionals are joining the management team, but the basis of the original vision will still remain.

The ROC is a place where rough sleepers and those in hostels and insecure accommodation can get something to eat, a shower, and a change of clothing. More importantly than this in many ways is that they receive the love of Christ.

Many of the people who use this project have drug or alcohol problems, mental health problems or are ex-offenders, so they are a difficult section of the homeless community to work with. The volunteers demonstrate sacrificial love, receiving very little in return, but it seems to me that this is what proclaiming the word of God by deed is all about. It does give people the chance to share their faith in an unthreatening way with those on the edge of society.

Robert Warren talks about different ways of being church.[6] The nearest example he gives to what is going on at ROC is that of people of different occupations getting together to give a Christian response in their own area of expertise. I think this is similar, but it was never planned. Rather it has evolved and matured from the grass roots, and this is one of its major strengths.

Loneliness is a big issue in many people's lives. In the same book Robert Warren comments on this and the breakdown in community, suggesting that the church could enter into this void in a missionary way. Loneliness is probably magnified if you are a homeless person feeling cold with little to eat. One indication of this is that a high number of the service users are ex-prisoners, and the first place they make for on release is the ROC, which they see as home. It is a place where they can sit in the warm and have other people around them, not just people in the same situation but also others who talk to them in a non-judgmental manner.

One example of this comes from Jim, who had been through the care system. He says that his foster parents really cared for him but he still felt an outcast and

---

6   Robert Warren, *Building Missionary Congregations* (Church House Publishing, 1995).

did not fit into society. At the early stages of the project, when the ROC was still on the car park, Jim was homeless, into crime and abusing drugs and alcohol. When he was encouraged to join the people from the ROC and offered something to eat, he thought there must be a catch. Jim now has a flat, has stopped using drugs and reduced his drinking. He says that without doubt if it had not been for the love and the beliefs of the people at ROC he would not have made it this far.

### Ground Rules and Boundaries

It is most important to have rules in place and to make it clear to the service users that these boundaries cannot be crossed. There is sometimes a danger that Christians feel they are there to take anything that is thrown at them. Not only is this not true, but if volunteers are in fear of verbal or physical abuse they will soon disappear from the project and the project will not be able to run. And service users needs to know where they stand, and often appreciate guidelines to help them grow and to develop.

Once the rules are established, effective sanctions for those crossing the line must be put in place and kept to. If people flout the rules and get away with it you lose the respect of those using the project. To exclude someone for a period of time is an effective sanction, and in extreme cases a permanent ban is necessary. People should not be afraid to call the police. In some quarters people see this as an unChristian thing to do but the safety of church workers and volunteers should be the first priority.

### Spiritual Needs

In the same way that material needs of people are met, so the ROC seeks to offer spiritual food. This needs to be tailored to the service user and so appropriate acts of worship have been produced. At harvest the gospel was presented by a multimedia presentation. The Christian Motorcyclists were present, and one who had been homeless and in prison gave his testimony. At Christmas there was a short act of worship shared by the Anglican Lay Chaplain of ROC and a deacon from the local Roman Catholic Church.

Another example of a drop-in centre is at the Whitechapel Centre in Liverpool. This is a secular project, but it has a high Christian ethos with some key Christians on its management committee. Revd Guy Elsmore, of Widnes, has been involved with the centre since 1989. His direct work has centred on the area of dying and bereavement counselling. This is what he had to say:

> Pat was a friendly, sometimes inebriated user of the Centre who burned to death in his bed-sit. The experience of sitting in a crematorium beside Pat's coffin, with Centre staff and clients, listening to an anonymous and inappropriate sermon, made me determined to play my part in helping the church to witness to God at these times among the homeless community. The death of a young rough sleeper, who went home to his family and their church for the funeral, left the Centre staff and clients feeling they had not mourned, so this

led to the first memorial service.

I was asked to be part of the service to officiate and preach, with the help of Centre staff. Someone read a poem that they had written; another Centre user had drawn a beautiful design for the order of service, a member of staff read from the Bible. We each wrote a prayer or a message for him. After these were read we burnt the papers as a symbolic offering of prayer. Hymns and prayers were used as they would be at any memorial service, and tea and biscuits were served afterwards.

The annual memorial service takes place in November at the initiative of Centre users and staff. I do not run it; I simply do what I am asked to do, which is usually to preach. I talk about the big things—life, death, memory and hope and as a Christian minister link them to the gospel.

Guy summed up in this way: 'When anyone conducts or attends a funeral or memorial service, we cannot help but reflect on our own mortality and the state of our lives. Often when homeless people die, their own family have not seen them for many years and the people who will miss them the most will be the people with whom they have shared a hostel dormitory, a cigarette, a bottle or a needle. Christian ministry among the homeless around the issue of death and bereavement is a matter of extreme sensitivity.' Any church that has links with homeless people needs to consider how they respond to this need. For further reading I would recommend the report *People not Paupers* by UNLEASH.[7]

### New Ways of Being Church

If we are serious about being church in a new way then it has to be more than words—it has to be matched by actions. I spoke to Revd Madeleine Bulman, a vicar in Shepherds Bush who runs a local church-based project called 'The Upper Room.' She stated that 'it is about removing the barriers that we expect homeless people to jump that we do not expect our normal congregations to jump.' One of these barriers is for homeless people to come into buildings unfamiliar to them for worship. It is about worshipping where they feel secure and it is following the example of Jesus and being incarnational among homeless people.

It is also about giving them a bridge between what they are familiar and unfamiliar with and helping them to worship God in their own way. A person who has either never or not for some time been to church may find it difficult to cope with our services. We must acknowledge this and look for alternatives.

However, I do feel there is a danger that a drop-in centre can become a comfort zone supporting people but not empowering them. There must be a clear structure in place to move people on and to help them into a home that is suitable to their own needs, and maybe also to help them find a spiritual home, in an existing congregation or in a new one.

---

7    UNLEASH, *People not Paupers* (Church Action on Homelessness in London October 1998, Trinity House, 4 Chapel Court, Borough High Street, London SE1 1HW).

# 6
# Hostels and Move-On Accommodation

For many people who are homeless the first type of accommodation they find can often be in a hostel. Once in a hostel, an individual plan to help each person can often be worked out.

Some people remain in the hostel system, forming another type of homelessness by moving from one hostel to another. But most hostels have a system in place to help the clients to establish themselves in independent living. Many homeless people live very chaotic lifestyles, often linked to drink and drugs, and so they need a lot of help and support. The move on from a hostel might be to a house with a number of bedsits with a high level of support, and then a move on to a flat of their own with a floating support worker who would help them maintain the tenancy.

Peter Parkinson and a group of Christian people in Leeds formed 'Caring for Life' as a registered charity in 1987. The Scripture that inspired them was Isaiah 58, 'Share your bread with the hungry and shelter the homeless poor'; this very much became their focus. The aim of the project is to share the love of Jesus with homeless and vulnerable young people in society by providing accommodation, work experience and long-term support, enabling them to develop dignity, self respect and to hear the gospel by word and deed.

They have two houses providing accommodation for eight people in each, one for men and one for women. The houses are intended for people who have been damaged by the past and need to be supported in a loving Christian environment.

Since the project started, 2,000 young people have been assisted through the residential homes or through placing in independent living accommodation. In addition to locating accommodation, they have gone a stage further by obtaining furniture and sometimes helping to decorate the property. This, together with long-term and twenty-four-hour support, seems to be a key to success—if the flat starts out in a poor condition it is very hard to take pride in it and to look after it.

When the person is in a new flat the project provides ongoing support and helps to build up the essentials of life that are needed: training in life skills such as basic hygiene, budgeting, cooking and cleaning, access to emergency help and—perhaps most important of all—friendship. Ninety people are presently being supported in this way through four paid floating support workers.

It may be that your church could not set up a project on this scale, but most churches could get involved in the mentoring of people who are going into their first tenancy. There would, of course, be a need to enter into partnership with a housing provider. Vetting and police checking of potential mentors would also be needed, together with supervision and support, but this would not be very expensive.

Within our churches there are vast untapped resources through the skills that people have developed in their own life journey, and as we build real relationships with people the gospel can be demonstrated through the love shown. As I said earlier, loneliness is a major problem for homeless people and also for those moving into their first tenancy. To be there for them simply as a friend is very valuable. Often the opportunity to share one's Christian faith will present itself.

This kind of mentoring programme is already being carried out by the Quakers in Bethnal Green, East London with a great deal of success. Volunteers are recruited and trained to deliver basic life skills to the tenants. They offer support for six months, and it would appear that this has enabled a good number of people to hold down a tenancy.

### Work Experience

'Caring for Life' also has a farm to give people work experience and day care. This is a key area because a number of homeless people have never worked and need constructive daytime activities. The Diocese of Liverpool has had some involvement with New Deal for 18–24 year olds in Merseyside. An extensive report has been written on this, *New Deal and the Diocese*[8] which is available from the Liverpool Diocesan Board for Social Responsibility, but one thing that became obvious to me was that a high level of motivation was needed.

*The Big Issue* does not feel that their vendors can move from selling the *Issue* to training for employment through New Deal. After long periods of homelessness or unemployment they are completely de-motivated. New Deal requires a full-time commitment which many of these people are simply not ready for, and to put them on such a scheme is setting them up to fail.

What is needed is perhaps an interim stage where they can gain access to work and training at a rate and level they are ready for. For example the *Big Issue in the North* in Manchester have computers which vendors can work on when they feel like it, and as they achieve then they can increase their involvement. The farm run by 'Caring for Life' would also seem to fulfil the same sort of role of moving people towards full-time employment.

Perhaps we as Christians, either as a church body or as individuals, can explore ways to help people to take this interim step. We must, however, be aware that at times we will be let down and used, and should be ready to take the pain that goes with that.

One way I have contributed to this is by taking people to the West Pelton Outdoor Activity Centre, which is run by Captain Alan Rainford of Church Army. We have taken eight residents and two staff members from projects, and engaged in climbing, raft building, and other pursuits. Not only do people develop by doing the activities but also it builds up relationships and the activities can be used to start up a formal discussion group. For example, with archery you can talk about hitting the target and maybe what we are aiming for in life, and if

---

8    Liverpool Diocese Board for Social Responsibility, *New Deal and the Diocese* (1999).

appropriate the point can be made that Jesus loves us whether we hit the target or not.

A spin-off from initiatives like this is that it shows the agencies that we have something a little bit different to offer. I have been fortunate enough to obtain funding for this piece of work, but within our churches there are people who are already qualified and able to deliver some, if not all, of these things. Whatever we offer, though, it is imperative that we provide a professional service, because secular agencies will judge us on what they see and will only work with us if our product is high quality.

Over the past thirteen years 'Caring For Life' has seen about three hundred people come to faith in Christ. Seekers services were started to provide a non-threatening and easily understood context for those who may never have entered a church in their lives, including those with literacy problems. The services have been a real blessing to those attending and most now attend the other church services as well.

Work like this must be approached with a long-term view. There will be no quick fix, or huge numbers coming to the Lord, but I do believe this to be what we have been commanded to do. It is part of our commission from Christ. John Stott puts it very well. He quotes from John 20.21: 'As the Father has sent me, I am sending you.' He then goes on to say that if our mission is based on the mission of Jesus it will surely involve us in entering into other people's worlds.[9]

The church does not run the charity 'Caring for Life,' and no formal acts of worship take place for the young people, but there are staff prayers and some young people do join in. 'Caring For Life' does not force the Christian faith onto anyone, but those involved share the gospel freely, encourage young people to attend church and nurture those who come to faith. This is a different approach from that used at the ROC. Many churches support 'Caring for Life' in prayer and 58% of their income comes from Christian people.

Staff members often invite people to their church, and it seems this is the bridge between the project and the church, that of personal relationship. The staff members are a mixture of paid and voluntary workers, but they are all Christians who are engaging with the world and demonstrating in a very professional way the love of Christ. These actions demonstrate the gospel.

The young people could easily feel alienated by the church services, but it seems that the seeker services are a tremendous method of introducing people to church. As they have observed a number of people have successfully crossed the bridge from project to church.

9   John Stott, *New Issues Facing Christians Today* (Marshall Pickering, 1999).

# 7
# Conclusion

Homeless people will be with us for the foreseeable future. In this booklet we have looked at several examples of how the church has responded to the needs of homeless people. From these examples we can see that there is no one model of working, but what does seem to be the common link is that all the projects made a response to a need in close consultation with other agencies and demonstrate a high level of professionalism.

There are also differences in the way that projects relate to the sponsoring church. In some instances the homeless project is part of the church activity and seen very much as part of the ministry of the church. But in other cases the project is quite separate, with its own project management and much looser connections with the church. When setting up a project the model that is being followed would need to be well thought through and the leadership of the church would need to be totally committed to the vision for either model to work. If there is not this strong link the project could move quite quickly to become a secular project, as many have in the past.

On a number of occasions we have reflected upon the question, 'is this a new way of being church?' There has been no common thread, but a desire to work with people on the edge and being prepared to accept them into the body of the church are of paramount importance. There is no disgrace in admitting that a fellowship is not yet ready to get involved in this sort of work, because more harm than good can be done if a piece of work is started too early. Individual members could join existing projects to gain experience.

It may be that the vision is correct but the timing is wrong and it is something for later on. Meanwhile other things without the same cost can be done. For example, the Mothers' Union in Liverpool has donated over a thousand toiletry bags in a year to homeless projects. This is the kind of thing that we can all do.

Jesus stated that the poor would always be with us and as Christians we must always be open to their need and ready to respond.

# 8
# Appendix: Useful Contacts

Shelter
88 Old Street
London
EC1V 9HU
Tel: 020 7 505 2000
http://www.shelter.org.uk

Catholic Housing Aid Society
209 Old Marylebone Rd
London NW1 5QT
Tel: 020 7 723 7273
info@chasnet.demon.co.uk
www.chasnet.demon.co.uk

Churches National Housing Coalition
Central Buildings
Oldham Street
Manchester
M1 1JT
Tel: 0161 236 9321
coalition@justhousing.co.uk

Caring For Life
Crag House Farm
Smithy Lane
Cookridge
Leeds
LS16 7NH
Tel: 0113 261 2131

Church Army
Marylebone Project
1-5 Cosway Street
London
NW1 5NR
Tel: 020 7 262 3818

Frontline Church
PO Box 38
Wavertree
Liverpool
L15 0FH
Tel: 0151 733 3373

The ROC
103 Church Street
St. Helens
Merseyside
WA10 1AJ
Tel: 01744 20032

Church Action on Poverty
Central Buildings
Oldham Street
Manchester
M1 1JT
Tel: 0161 236 9321

Quaker Social Action
Bunhill
Fields Meeting House
Quaker Court
Banner Street
London EC1Y 8QQ
Tel: 020 7 250 1193

Liverpool Diocese Board for Social
Responsibility
Church House
1 Hanover Street
Liverpool L1 3DW
Tel: 0151 709 5586
Fax: 0151 709 7596